# A TEMPORARY STATE OF GRACE

MEDITATIONS BY DAVID S. BLANCHARD

Skinner House Books
Boston

FOR JULIA AND EMILY

# CONTENTS

Beginnings and endings always seem to capture our imagination and attention. Beginnings and endings hold some secrets that we are forever wanting to reveal. Beginnings and endings give a degree of definition to our lives, and when we encounter reminders of these book-ends of life, we can't help but remember something of our own beginnings and wonder about our own endings.

Beginnings and endings have a magic and a mystery that cause us to stop and listen. When we are in the presence of such moments of transformation, when we publicly and collectively welcome a baby to the world or grieve a death, when we privately mark the parting with a friend or the re-birth of someone's spirit, we feel ourselves drawn into a profound and compelling encounter with the most vital and real dimensions of life.

Whenever we witness something of a birth or a death, a part of us knows we too share in that moment. In it a part of us may die a little. In it a part of us could be born again.

Once upon a time someone held us when we were born. And someday, someone somewhere will mourn us and miss us. And in between those times, we move through the seasons of life, and step back and forth through memory and imagination, from what was our beginning to what will be our end.

SUMMER'S END

In spite of the ninety degree days, all signs point to summer's end. The last fling of summer will arrive with Labor Day picnics and excursions, with the packing up at cottages, with final swims in the lake, or last days at the beach. Each of us will find something to savor when the temperature is closer to nine degrees than ninety.

But even before the last stand of summer, the shape of the season has already begun to change. Emily Dickinson wrote, "How softly summer shuts, without the creaking of a door." Of the sounds that summer brings to the world, I always think of the sound of a screen door slapping shut as one of the ways that summer announces its presence. It's a sound that Emily Dickinson would have heard, a sound that most of us grew up hearing, yet one that my daughter Emily may not come to associate with summer. Screen doors today slide or close gently thanks to modern technology. Summer does not end with such sharpness, but with a subtlety that we might barely notice.

Even now, leaves have begun to drop from trees, green and brittle. Gardens are about ready to give up. Sunflowers slouch as if they'd like to lie down and rest a while. And of course, the light is changing. The shadows come earlier, and stretch out longer across the lawns. We humans begin our short migration indoors. It happens. It's already begun.

Before it's really over, I hope to listen for the slapping of a few screen doors that will remind me that summer still reigns, but also to be still enough to sense the end of this time we call summer, and to know just "how softly summer shuts."

# A CALL TO WORSHIP

Come down off the ladder.
Wash out that paint brush.
Shake the sand out of your shoes.
Get up off your muddy knees,
and give the garden a morning off.
Fold up the newspaper.
Turn off the coffee pot.
Close up your calendar,
already filled with dates,
and times,
and people,
and places that claim you.
This church is ready for you to fill its rooms,
to create its spirit, to generate its warmth,
to kindle its light.
This church is ready for you to make community,
to create beauty, to bend it toward justice,
to serve its ideals.
This church is ready for you to be here,
honoring our past,
invigorating our present,
and dreaming our future.
This is your church.
Here we are home.
Here we are whole.
Let us begin.

If a perfect church existed (and I have it on good authority that one has yet to develop), I think it would resemble something like the perfect home—another institution that lives more in our imaginations than in practice. There are obvious differences of course. One usually joins a family by no choice of one's own. At home members may receive an allowance; at church it works the other way around. At home, unlike at church, the leaders actually have some power to enforce their authority, even if it's only because they are bigger or older. Yet we persist in speaking about *being at home in church*. This is what this ideal means to me:

I hope this home will be a place of shelter, a refuge from the tumult of life's disappointments and defeats, a place of consolation and encouragement.

I hope this home will be a place of challenge, not complacency, a space where we are helped to mature and take on a wider sense of responsibility for ourselves and others.

I hope this home will be a place where we can be ourselves, unencumbered by judgments or ridicule, where we are accepted as we are, where we are, and for whom we are.

I hope this home will be a place we might take some risks, knowing that there will be arms to catch us if we fall.

I hope we will know this home as a place of love,

6  where life is made whole, where we may become engaged at the deepest levels of being alive.

If we give these hopes life among us in the community that is found at church, then there will be no place quite like it, and we will know that we are home.

"Amazing Grace" is, without a doubt, the most popular hymn among the devout as well as among people who would tell you they're not a bit religious. In a documentary I saw about the importance of this one hymn in our culture, people kept using the word "amazing" to describe the song's impact on them. Performers, clergy, the young and the old, blacks, whites, British Anglicans, and Southern Baptists—all could go no further than the first word of the song to describe their feelings.

A fair amount of myth and mystery surrounds the actual events that may have put pen to paper to create this hymn, but this much is known. The author John Newton was active in the slave trade between West Africa and England in the nineteenth century. Arlo Guthrie likes to tell that Newton had a revelation and turned a loaded ship around to return to Africa. That probably didn't happen. What we do know is that his written accounts of the slave trade were instrumental in bringing about the abolition of slavery in England. He experienced a turning of the heart that led him to a life of service in the Church of England. And he wrote a hymn about what it means to experience transformation.

Most of us know something about spiritual transformation. We know the isolation of being lost and the feeling of wonder at being found. We each, in ways no one else may be able to notice, have passed "through many dangers, toils, and snares." The grace that leads us home will take many forms and will present itself in the guise of experiences we would never request. Grace just sneaks up on us and often steals away before we know what happened. Sometimes a single tear is what tells us. Sometimes a feeling of calm. It could be a lump in the throat. It could take the shape of laughter. Grace is something you can't demand. Grace is sometimes beyond understanding. But from time to time it pays us each a visit. Amazing.

I have learned a lot in the time since I came out as a gay man. Some joyful, some painful. I have felt isolated from some and closer to others. Of some things I have become more accepting, and of others, far less patient. In America I have learned what it is like to step out of straight, white privilege. All of this came into focus for me during the debates about the motives and messages of the Million Man March in Washington, DC.

Like most other white people, I find Minister Farrakhan to be a frightening character. He is blatantly anti-Semitic and homophobic. His brand of patriarchy is a remnant from another century. During the creation of the Million Man March, his appeal to black rage didn't strike me as "constructive" to easing racial tension, so it was easy for me to sympathize with white people who opposed any gathering led by a demagogue like him.

The only problem I saw was that Minister Farrakhan didn't create the rage or despair that blacks experience. These existed with or without him. He was simply the leader of a massive public witness to our nation's neglect of the scourge of racism that lives at the core of our culture. Between the reaction to the O. J. Simpson verdict, the murder of Jonny Gammage, and the Million Man March, October 1995 may well be recorded as one of the most racially divisive times since the sixties.

Or maybe these events simply pulled back the concealing curtain. In retrospect, the March in Washington was a peaceful, orderly demonstration of solidarity and support among men of the African-American community. The stereotype of the shiftless black man was revealed untrue by this show of purpose, conviction, and commitment. White opposition to the March gives evidence that oppression is perpetuated in subtle ways.

I supported the March because, to a far less restrictive degree, I stand in a minority that some hold as despised. I know why black men had to march, even under Farrakhan's bombastic banner. They marched, not so much to demonstrate something to others, but to show it to themselves. They marched to affirm their humanity and against the messages of a culture that demeans them. They marched to celebrate their survival in a world that has historically considered them fair targets for hatred and violence. They marched to encourage one another in the unfinished struggles, personal and political, that lie ahead.

As a white man, this is what I think.

As a gay man, this is what I know.

If it had been left up to me, which I am glad it was not, I probably would have stayed in Europe when my multitude of ancestors were leaving France, England, Wales, and Germany. I would have waved goodbye from the dock and asked them to write. When it comes to drawing the line between the settlers and the pioneers of this world, I usually find myself with those who stay home, bidding farewell from the edge of town at the end of the pier to the more adventuresome pioneers. Neither characteristic is better or worse than the other, but I suspect that each of us would know where we belong. We need both types, even while we feel resentful or jealous of the other's way of life. The damn pioneers drag us off in unknown directions, and the damn settlers dig in their heels and won't budge. But is that all they do?

Where would we be in this world without the pioneers? (I would be a coal-miner in Wales.) Where would we be without people who explore new territories of the world or the mind? (I might be writing with a quill pen.) Where would we be without people who give life its stability, or risk the uncertainty of change? What would life be like without the security fostered by the settlers or the innovations dreamed up by the pioneers? We may drive each other crazy, but I'm coming to understand that I need the pioneers as much as they need me to keep life in balance, and to keep the home fires burning.

Not too long ago I was signing in at a local hospital when I noticed something that had escaped me before. While checking to see if the parishioner I had come to visit had been transferred to another room, I saw that in the clergy register she had been transferred to another denomination: "other."

I can think of three good reasons why the hospital should move us out to the margins of "otherdom." For one, there are twenty-one letters in our merged Unitarian Universalist name. "Other" is short, with only five.

Then there is the fact that in numbers we account for something less than an asterisk of the total population. When you put all us "others" together, we account for something, perhaps even a majority.

Last, though we religious liberals are sometimes loath to admit it, we often find some degree of comfort in our obscurity. You know, "if you were properly progressive and open minded, you'd know who we were, and if you don't, well then we're not so sure you belong here."

In the nineteenth century the liberal Christians in the Congregational Church adopted as their own the pejorative name given them by the orthodox. They accepted and became organized around the name Unitarian. During my hospital visit, my parishioner and I laughed a bit about the possibilities should our congregation become known as the "First Other Church." A good graphic artist could easily fashion a chalice design inside the "O" for our logo. People who heard our new name would likely be more curious than confused. The modest two syllables of "other" would certainly be easier than the ten we currently use. We could, collectively, save much breath. I personally think the people who fashioned the merger of 1961 could have made matters much simpler had they found a shorter and more meaningful name for the new Association of congregations. But, for reasons that probably made sense at the time, they didn't. In the big picture, this is not a problem. What we are about as a religious movement is far more important than what we are called.

But there is some level at which I'm not comfortable being the minister of an "other" religion. Other than what? That we are different from many orthodox expressions of faith, I can accept and affirm. But the notion that we "others"—be we Unitarian Universalists, Ba'hai's, Muslims, Friends, etc.—are less than, diminished, marginalized because of our differences or differentness, is something I won't accept. We are an alternative path *for* spiritual understanding and religious expression; we are not an alternative *to* those grounding endeavors.

Our work together is in finding ways to extend the understanding and practice of liberal religion—in our own lives, in the lives of our communities, and maybe even in the lives of those who decide who's a "who," and who's an "other."

Something happened the other day that has made me wonder if maybe machines are not only smarter than people, but wiser. The machine in question is my office computer.

There are many things it can do that I cannot, and probably never will. My computer has a memory that exceeds anything I could ever hope for. It remembers things I would rather it (and I) could forget: half-baked sermons, memos about old problems, letters I wished I hadn't sent. It's all there. Billions of bytes of information preserved until I can figure out how to send them to that big deletion in the sky.

Besides having a memory that runs circles around me, it's a mean speller. (I'm not.) Thier? Their? Friend? Freind? I know the rules. I was present in third grade: "I" before "e" except after "c," etc., etc., etc. The fact that *I* knew what *I* meant didn't impress my earliest teachers. My computer doesn't mark off for spelling, and for that I am grateful.

But about the smart computer being wise. I was proofing a document and the spell-checker came back to me with the message "Not found." The word was misery. M-I-S-E-R-Y. Hmm. Does it require an "a" instead of an "e"? No. I had actually spelled it correctly. "Nice work, David," I thought. Outsmarting the computer! Then I began to think about it.

What's the message here? What's this business, "Not found"?

Could it be that misery really does love company, usually ours? Could it be that we sometimes go looking for it to give ourselves some strange sense of companionship? What would happen if we stopped looking? Or started to look for something else? What if our brains came back to us with the message "Not found" the next time we sought the company of misery? Maybe, just maybe, my computer was giving me the message I needed to hear. I think I'll leave misery alone, and hope it won't find me either.

We've all been to someone's house where saying grace is a mandatory practice before the meal. It's not always a comfortable moment, and not because it's a grace but because it is mandatory. In my experience, it seems these mandatory graces are divided into a couple of categories. The first is the "sectarian blessing." For example, this one might be addressed to the (your faith here) God to make the meal suitable and sustaining to the (your faith here) people around the table. These blessings make me nervous. The second category is the "speed-reading blessing," spoken so quickly that you have no clue what was said. These make me dizzy. And then there are those occasions where the host or hostess can't resist asking me, a minister, to offer a professional prayer over the pot roast. These usually make me feel inept.

If there is ever a time of year when dining rooms all over America set a place at the table for religion, it's at Thanksgiving. As anachronistic as it may feel, some sort of prayer can be a meaningful ritual by which we might acknowledge the blessings of human companionship and love, the sustenance and strength derived from the earth, and the magic and mystery of our relationship to Creation. It's big stuff. It's there without our having created it or without our having invoked it. It's sitting right there beside us. It seems, at the very least, that we might give a nod in its direction, and recognize all we have been given, unbidden.

My Thanksgiving blessing is already figured out. It'll be the same one my family uses every time we sit at the table together. But it's not a prayer I lead. I have a young zealot that set our tradition in place. When she was three, my daughter Emily must have been to a friend's house where they said a prayer before eating. She returned home, took our hands, and said, "Praise! Praise!" So that is what we started to do. We share some part of our day that we were thankful for. It's rarely profound, and occasionally silly. But we do it anyway, being reminded, even on a bad day, that there is much to praise. I recommend it. Emily recommends it. Let us praise.

Forgiving is a somewhat reckless, typically illogical act. A leap of faith, if you will. When Jesus preached forgiveness, people thought he was insane. Loving your neighbor is one thing, but your enemies too? When struck on one cheek, offer the other? If someone takes your coat, give your cloak as well? We may think it was easy for Jesus to say this, his father being God and all. But what about those of us who live in the real world? Do we have to do it too?

I suppose it depends on what we want from life. Forgiveness in the world is still a bit reckless and illogical. But so is love, having children, or creating anything that we are willing to give away. But we do these things all the time, and we trust that because we have done them, we will be more fulfilled, more connected, more present to the joys and wonders of the world. The alternative is to be satisfied with dismal little corroded existences. But most of the time, we rarely make a conscious choice between the two.

It is through forgiveness that we can discover the freedom it takes to place ourselves in right relation to the divine, with those we love and care about, and with ourselves. It may not be logical, but forgiveness—clear and unconditional—frees the forgiver more deeply than the person being forgiven. Chances are good they didn't even know they had done something that required forgiving. It's a bold and constructive step based in a sense of faith that forgiveness withheld is a poison to the soul. When we hold back forgiveness, we repeat over and over our hurt, reassuring ourselves of our indignation. Some people live their lives off that pain. It's not required. Real power and authentic freedom come with what is so hard to do: forgive.

In the end, those who have found a way to forgive know that the most profound work of forgiveness is done not for those who want it, but for the sake of mending our own soul and for the freedom we find when we recklessly squander our forgiveness.

A group of us recently spent an hour and a half considering the power of words—in particular, religious language. For Unitarian Universalists, words are about as close as we come to having a *sacrament* (n. something regarded as sacred). And because we come from widely varied religious (and non-religious) traditions, we do not bring a common understanding of traditional religious terms. Despite the fact that we all speak the same language, some words strike some people as deeply comforting and, at the same time, strike others like fingernails on a blackboard. Yes, it matters that we might understand each other better. But more important, I think the value of our discussions have been to acknowledge that we have misplaced something significant in our worship of words. We have neglected the deeper and fuller realities that words only represent in the smallest of fragments. Take prayer for example.

Many of us would probably say we do not *pray* (n. to implore, to ask, of God). End of discussion. But is it? What shall we call those generous moments in our existence when we blurt out, to no one in particular, "thank you"? What is it we are doing when we utter words of desolation when the spirit of life has somehow forsaken us? It is thought. It is speech. It is feeling. But is it a prayer?

Out of gratitude, or out of grief, there is an encounter with a sense that we alone did not create our good fortune, or that we alone cannot walk out of the darkness. Shall these stammerings, directed to the mystery of the universe, be called prayer? What if no one is listening?

I'd suggest that the most essential listening "being" is tuned in when such intentions fill our consciousness. And that person is ourselves. These sorts of intentions are about our listening to our life. These sorts of intentions transform each of us by virtue of their fundamental and urgent honesty. As such, we could call them just about anything. The word doesn't matter much. What matters is the manner in which our encounter with the mystery motivates us to live and be in the world. So our prayers might be more a function of our attitude than an isolated act on bended knee.

There are many ways to be born again, hopefully not just once or twice. To keep up with the little deaths that come with the passing of time, we ought to get born again as much as time allows. Don't hang around though for God to tap you on the shoulder. Live in the anticipation that it's about to happen at any second, because that's the way it'll be. You'll be reading a book, or listening to some music, when some part of life will suddenly make more sense. You'll awake from a dream and know something you hadn't known before. You'll be making love, or cooking, or carving a pumpkin with a child, or painting, and you will be aware of participating in the creation of something that exists apart from you, and as a part of you at the same time.

There will be times when we all live as exiles. Gay or straight. Believer or nonbeliever. Young or old. Healthy or ill. Brilliant or average. Rich or poor. But the time comes when we are invited to follow a path of reconciliation with all that has been scattered and separated from us. The exile in us can have a long, long way to travel. Some will not go: isolated by hurt, indifferent from disappointment, alienated by anger.

But I don't believe that any of that is the plan. I believe, as surely as I believe anything, that in this life, everything is possible. That is not to say that we will have everything we want, or need, or deserve, but that our souls, the most essential and real dimension of our being, are not confined by the restrictions of the past or the limits of the imagined future. Sometimes that means we live, simply, in hope and trust that the time of renewal, of rebirth, is yet to come. But that it will come if we are alive and aware and receptive.

We have been created to be free.
We have been created to know joy.
We have been created to love.
We were not made to be exiles.

MEMORIAL PRAYER FOR A COLLEAGUE

Great Spirit,
welcome us in prayer.

Our time together has been enriched by the expressions of memory.

Stories have been told, gifts have been affirmed, foibles embraced. Images have been created out of the store of shared experiences. Some of who he was has been re-membered.

May our prayer be to honor all that has been forgot-ten. Let us shape a prayer of gratitude for the fragments no one is left to remember. Let us be the ones who give thanks for the little things too insignificant to recall. Let us listen in this quiet for what has not been said.

We pray for a vision of all that is forgotten:
For words that healed and for gestures that embraced,
For mistakes that were made and for mercy that
    was shown,
For wisdom earned and for disappointments born,
For sacrifices endured and for love that was lost,
For loyalty unreturned and for faith rewarded.

Our prayer is one of gratitude for the forgiveness that is hidden in forgetting, the forgiving and forgetting of our human stumblings by those who know us best.

For this life now ended, and for our own sake, may we know that even what has been forgotten is never lost. It has been changed by time into something new we can no longer recognize, but that we somehow know. In the silence, let us remember some of what has been forgotten.

Amen.

This is a time of year when we ask—and are asked—what do you want? Shall it be another tie, a new pair of gloves, a book? We ask and we answer. We shop, we wrap, we ship. And the season usually comes and goes without us ever really answering the question: *What do you want?*

Some of the things we want we might be afraid to ask for because we can't be sure what we would do if we got them. Many things we want we don't know enough to ask for. Most things we can't ask for because we know no one can give them to us.

Most people ask the question without any interest in really knowing, yet it can be a question for each of us to hold on to for a time in mind and heart. What do we want? Not what would we like, but what do we want to give us a deeper connection with life and to help us give expression to our love? Not a long list of things, but a sense of clarity that illuminates what it is we are doing and why. Not outward signs of generosity, but an internal sense of caring that guides us to give in any season. Not just the reflex of always giving, but also the courage to truly answer some of those people who ask us, "What do you want?"

Dare to answer. Think of the things you want, and the things that others close to you would want. Imagine the ways they might be given and received.

What do you want?

Sometimes I think I can teach my children things that will make life better for them as they grow up. I want to believe I can protect them, or that there is some way for me to do their learning for them. This line of thinking is routinely flawed, not because my children are poor learners, but because I'm not always the best teacher. Despite my efforts to avoid repeating mistakes, I'm still learning things I thought I knew. Just last year I mistook a gift for a present.

This gift was a homemade potholder woven of colorful scraps of cloth. It wasn't perfect. It wasn't beautiful. It wasn't particularly unusual. Accepting it as a present, I placed it into service beside the stove.

Four days before Christmas I was called to officiate at a memorial service for a friend. Talking with her five- and nine-year-old daughters, I asked what things they liked to remember about their mom. What things did they do together? What had she taught them? They were busy, deep at work on a gift-making project, but they expressed some memories that mattered, and recounted some gifts their mother had shared with them: making cookies . . . snuggling in bed . . . being their Brownie leader . . . planting bulbs. Then the nine year old looked down and said, "And she taught us how to make these potholders!"

Of course! A gift! How could I miss it?

Presents are the sort of things that fit on lists, complete with size and color preference. Presents are the sorts of things we are smart enough to ask for. Gifts are altogether different. We don't usually think to ask for them, perhaps because we think we don't deserve them, or don't want to risk expressing the need. Maybe we don't even recognize the need ourselves. Gifts differ from presents because no matter what form they take, they always represent something greater, something deeper, something more enduring; they are about things like love, respect, and affirmation.

Gifts given are often woven into some simple token. And sometimes, protecting our own comfort, we give them in disguise. They can be easy to miss.

Now I try to give more gifts than presents, and without too much camouflage. Be gift-bearers yourselves. Give them along with presents, and look carefully for the gifts others are trying to give you.

I write this, and you will read it, at the start of a "new" year. I say "new," because that is how it has been parceled out in the proper number of days and weeks and months to make a year. One is over. One is beginning. For the next couple of weeks we will all persist in writing the wrong year on checks and letters. Quickly, the new year will become simply this year, and the old year will become attached to all that's past.

To me, New Year's Eve has always seemed a rather arbitrary festival. A grand excuse for a good party. A useful time for reflection. An occasion for resolutions to be made, or at least toyed with, for the future. I don't subscribe to the notion of time that the new year traditionally promotes, with the old geezer being shown the door as the young tyke in diapers makes her entrance. I think that time accumulates for each of us, and that the slate is never made blank. It's more like a mural that we keep adding panels to, bending around the corners of our lives.

There are such things as "new years" in all of our lives. But rarely do I think they begin and end according to the Roman calendar. They begin and end, at times by choice and at times by chance, at rather arbitrary moments of transformation. Perhaps in a moment of loss. Other times when we feel in control of our lives and make a decision to live differently. Maybe in that rare moment when we know we are in love. Or when we begin a new job, have a baby, write a poem, change our mind, get sick, lose a friend, look in a mirror. You'll know the time. You'll know when your own "new year" has begun. When it happens, raise a toast, throw confetti, wear a funny hat, blow on a noisemaker. It'll be time to mark. Even if it's July. Especially if it's July. Happy New Year, whenever.

Even the most rational of religions cannot live without myths. A dangerous one among Unitarian Universalists is that we are somehow better than everyone else. Smarter. More sophisticated. More progressive. Better traveled. Smarter. More humane. Wiser. Accomplished in the professions. Did I say smarter?

We like to list the famous folks who were Unitarian or Universalist throughout history: presidents, statesmen, artists, literary figures, social reformers, and the like. This, I know, is meant to impress. Maybe it's really just another way we oppress the vast multitudes of folks who find living the most ordinary lives a supreme accomplishment. For that reason, I'm advocating we remember the Unitarian Millard Fillmore.

The thirteenth President of the United States was born January 7, 1800 in Moravia, New York, and Moravia is proud of it. It's unlikely that Moravia will send forth another President, even a bad one, so they are trying to make the best of things. Millard Fillmore is generally acknowledged to be one of the worst Presidents we have had, remembered primarily for installing the first bathtub in the White House and promoting the pro-slavery Compromise of 1850. Leaving him off our litany of liberal lights isn't so much a disservice to him, as it is a distortion of our self-understanding as a human community about our capacity to be something less than perfectly astounding people.

I don't think I will go around promoting liberal religion to newcomers as the faith of Millard Fillmore. That would be like selling Fords by advertising a new model with the line, "From the people who brought you the Edsel . . ." But on the other hand, I think I'll be more careful about how much I name-drop as a means of validating the integrity of our faith. It can belong to anyone, and is neither the cause for their greatness, nor is it shamed by human struggle and failure.

Millard Fillmore is a good person for us to remember. Not just because he was Unitarian. Not just because he was the President. But because when we claim him as our own, we are also affirming something within ourselves that is unencumbered by shame and undaunted by disappointment. When we accept poor Millard, we are accepting our own ordinariness, our own mistakes, our own flaws. Because if we let Millard count, then there are good reasons why we should count too.

I am a collector. Not really of specific things, but of things in general. This is not a generalized trait in the Blanchard family, but rather one that has struck some of us, and one that has left others untouched. In my generation, I seem to be the carrier of this gene. My collections range from things that have value—such as antique church stuff like collection baskets, communion serving pieces, etc.—to things that are as ordinary as stones. (Well, they *are* stones.)

The church garage sale is for me a source of great temptation. When I should be donating that suit I bought for my first job sixteen years ago, I'm afraid it will be I going home with someone's slightly worn but cozy sports jacket. I should be thinning out my book collection, but I will be unable (I know) to resist what others have managed to part with.

There probably is some profound psychological reason for my behavior. In her first novel *The Book of Ruth*, Jane Hamilton made these remarks about the residents of Honey Creek, a fictional Midwestern town: "If you look in the garages you'll see that they're filled with rusty farm machines, milk cans, large rusted wagon wheels with broken spokes, from the ancestors. People in Honey Creek like to keep junk in the family. You never know if a huge chest of bent nails might not come in handy some time; you can't be too careful. I think folks hold on to metal scraps and furniture because the world is an enormous place, far and wide, but they have never experienced much of it, and they're afraid. They want an anchor so there's no danger of drifting away into outer space, or down under the ground, strange places they aren't too familiar with."

A part of me, I suspect, is from Honey Creek. It is the nostalgic part that wants to be able to hold on to what has long ago departed. It is the fearful part of me that at times prefers the anchor to the sail. But a part of me, a part I am more and more trusting of, is not from Honey Creek, and finds it claustrophobic. It is the part that wants to step on the gas as I approach that town. We might never get to travel to the world's "strange and unfamiliar places" if we are too busy holding on to our "chests of bent nails," in whatever incarnation we possess them.

I don't imagine that I will ever be without a certain amount of clutter in my life. (Just to grab onto if a big gust comes up.) But in this case, I think less could be more. So my resolution this year will be to bring more things to the sale than I take home. And besides, if I realize I have parted with something I can't live without, the chances are better than even that whoever buys it will bring it back for next year's sale.

Most of us look for love in only the most obvious places, and as a result, most of us come away disappointed. It's as if we are still grade school kids, counting valentines as a measure of what matters. The love that matters is not typically the subject of sonnets or love songs.

There can be love in being told we are wrong. There can be love in sharing a regret. There can be love in asking for help. There can be love in communicating hurt. There can be love in telling hard truths. Most of us find it painful to live at this level of love, but it can be there, even in these most unlikely places. It isn't the kind of love we've been promised in the fairy tales of princes and fairy godmothers, but it is the kind experienced by frogs and dwarfs. It's the sort of love that can bring us closer to finding the missing pieces of ourselves that we need to make us whole.

Some of the most loving things I've ever experienced, I haven't been ready for, wasn't looking for, and nearly didn't recognize. A few of them I didn't want. But all of them have changed me, transformed some part of me, filled in a place that I didn't even know was empty.

When the valentine has been tucked away in a drawer, the candy eaten, the flowers faded and gone, there will be other legacies of love that will last as long as we do, because they have brought us to know an element of life—part feeling, part idea, part mystery—that once known, is ours to keep.

I'm not sure why we say that we keep secrets, when in fact it's the other way around. They keep us. What family doesn't have a few kicking around? Affairs, abortions, suicides, alcoholism, mental illness, and other assorted indiscretions that lead someone to say in hushed tones, "Don't tell a word of this to anyone!" People have been known to survive hearing about all of those secrets, although more than a few have suffered from the anxiety, guilt, and shame of protecting a part of who they are from being known.

I've learned that every secret must, and will, become known. Perhaps the content of the secret will stay hidden, but surely the process of concealment reveals its own truth. The secret may remain whole, but the rest of a person's life starts to become distorted by the efforts to absorb the secret into their relationship with the world. In this way, there really are no secrets. They are given expression even in the fullest silence.

We all have them. For a number of years mine was that I was gay. It took me lots of time and turmoil to see the price I paid for pretending. Secrets can be a kind of sickness, and we convince ourselves that the cure is worse than the illness. But if the truth hurts, we must acknowledge that it can also heal. It makes us more authentic when we find the courage to trust that there is at our core a sense of worth that other people don't get to take away from us because they don't like us, or approve of us, or just don't care about us.

Consider the secrets you keep. Consider the ways that your secrets keep you. Scatter them if you can. Keep them if you must. Just don't try to forget them. If you do, you will lose track of who you are, where you've been, and where you would like to go. Secrets will tell themselves unless we find a way to do it for ourselves.

There may be several possible answers to why the Unitarian Universalist might cross the road. Among them: because that's where they were serving coffee; they didn't cross it, they transcended it; or that they only got as far as the middle of the road since they didn't want to take sides. The fact is that we "cross the road" for the same reason the chicken did: to get to the other side.

Getting to the other side isn't always simple. People we love die. We grow and change in unexpected ways. We make mistakes and hurt people we care about, and vice versa. We can find ourselves more alone at times than we think we can bear. And yet there are times when we are overwhelmed by the beauty of this world or by the blessing of unexpected kindness.

Getting to the other side is made easier when we choose to travel with others. Life in community isn't always easy, but it's the only place we can practice being human.

Finding our way to the other side is less treacherous when we listen and learn from those who have made the trip before and who know something about the route: Jesus, Buddha, and Zoroaster; Rumi, Starhawk, and Thoreau; Harriet Tubman, Malcolm X, and Harvey Milk. Teachers whose living was, and remains, a testament to the sacred dimensions of being human.

We will reach the other side with fewer regrets, and with less baggage, if we have found a way to accept each other for who we are, even as we seek to be who we might become. In community we are reminded of our ideals, yet it is also a place to confess our limitations and express our deepest hope.

Liberal religion is not "easy street," but what we do have to offer is this: a tradition that affirms human dignity, that encourages spiritual growth and discovery, and that is intellectually honest in the face of the complexities of our time. We offer these tools and our companionship so that we might help each other get safely from here to the other side.

A new record was set the other day. An old teddy bear was sold at auction for $65,000. It was made in the 1930s and a gentleman wished to give it to his wife for her birthday, the teddy bear and the wife being the same age. The pre-auction estimate was $1,000.

A romantic might respond "how sweet of that man to spend the equivalent of the gross national product of Burundi on a gift for his wife." A cynic might think less of the expenditure.

Most teddy bears accrue their value to their owners in direct proportion to the amount they are cuddled and hugged, slept with, cried upon, dragged about, and otherwise treasured. The teddy bear in the auction sold for $65,000 because it had never been touched. For over fifty years it sat in a box.

Now, I'm sure that poor teddy bear will get a lot of attention. It'll probably live in a display case and have its own insurance policy. But it'll never know the purposes for which it was created. It'll never be loved. For all those years, overlooked and forgotten. And forevermore, too valuable to be loved.

One could disparage the values of a society in which such extravagance exists. One could conclude that the owners confirm the wisdom that a fool and his money are soon parted. But the more I think about it, all I can think is, poor bear.

"I'm sorry to be writing you such a long letter.
I didn't have time to write a short one."
        —E. B. White, in a letter to a friend

I'm one of the last of the great letter writers. People frequently tell me what a wonderful correspondent I am. This usually from people who never write back, but pick up the phone on occasion. Yet I keep writing in the hopes that someone other than Ed McMahon will write.

The technology of phone calls and letters determines the sort of expression that they are best at delivering. Phone calls are transmitted. The voice is broken down into a scattering of signals, and then reassembled as other words flow past us. Letters, written words, by their nature are solid. Letters are slow and plodding. They clutter up desks. They are stories where phone calls are signals. We live by both, even if we have gotten a lot more accustomed to just sending out signals into the void, rather than struggling to narrate what it means to look into the void, to be faithful to the human predicament, to occupy the silences with the voice of our imagination.

The silences of phone calls are quickly filled; they can seem almost dangerous. But the silences of a letter can be fertile and nurturing. Some of those silences come from the writer, as an idea struggled with, and some are created by the readers who can proceed at their own speed into the new territory unfolded before them.

Long or short, letters are invitations into the interior of life in a way that a phone call can rarely match. I suppose I keep writing as a means of understanding where I have been and where I am going. When I add "please write" to a letter, I really mean it. If time is short, a long letter would be fine.

I'm well loved. That's usually a blessing and a comfort to me. Parents and daughters, lovers and friends, parishioners and colleagues, have shown me many signs of love in all its many guises: gratitude, passion, trust, and comfort. I'm lucky that way, and a more secure man might leave well enough alone. There's just one problem. I've worked long and hard through my life to earn that love. So I've wondered at times where would I be without it?

I really wondered about it when I was coming out. What would become of this carefully constructed world built upon such a deception? Who would love me when I found it so hard to love myself? I learned that God would love me.

Up until then, I had no clue what it meant to experience God's love. If someone told me "God loves you," I would smile outside and feel dismissed inside. And then one day, it was there. God's love. I knew that I was going to be okay. And it didn't depend on my congregation, my family, or my friends. It wasn't a love I had to earn or deserve. It was simply mine, and I felt filled with a kind of peace that the world could neither give nor take away. I call that God's love.

I believe it's there for all of us. Sometimes it needs a place of brokenness to get through. God's love needs the kind of space we create, in spite of our fears, when we are willing to allow what is most authentic about ourselves to be known. When the essence of the one meets the essence of all, it's love at first sight. God loves us for all the right reasons. As for what those reasons are, God only knows.

She comes home from kindergarten saying that he keeps kissing her. She comes home saying he's giving her love letters. She comes home saying he won't stop calling her "honey." No, this isn't testimony from some Senate hearing on sexual harassment. It's about my daughter and a little boy at school.

I suppose that this is not sexual harassment, but nonetheless, she doesn't like it. Some people would say that this is typical behavior for children this age, but it is only typical because it mirrors something that they see and hear from the culture that shapes their view of the world. It is a culture that has already given a little girl the feeling that a boy has power she does not have. It is a culture that has given a little boy confusing messages about the boundaries between the genders. Neither of them were taught these lessons on purpose. There are lots of "teachers" in the world that make subtle impressions we can't detect until they have been made.

The kindergarten teacher has talked to the children about respect. I've talked to my daughter about the very basic right she holds to stop someone from doing things that bother her, even things that other people think are cute. I feel okay about the resolution to this small drama, even if I'm discouraged about how such conflicts are often resolved in schools, work places, and government. The little boy may grow up to be on the Supreme

Court, despite this small blemish to his record. But then again, maybe Julia will be better qualified, having learned the harder lesson of having to fight for a freedom rather than giving up a privilege. All that, she learned in kindergarten.

I confess. I went to the new mega-grocery store that just opened on the east side of town. I went on the opening day to what's been promoted as the largest grocery store in this part of the state. I saw cars streaming in on my way to church in the morning, and they were still flocking in when I was on my way home at the end of the day. I usually avoid those crowd scenes, but by 9:00 p.m. the coast was clear. The frenzy appeared over.

I began my tour with a cup of coffee. I contemplated buying bread crumbs so I could leave a trail back to the parking lot. I passed first through acres of produce. Then down aisles paved with prepared foods. There was more bread stacked up there than most third world nations see in a month. You could buy any one of several kinds of seaweed, and exotic mushrooms could be had for $20 a pound. They have thirty-four checkout lanes, a dry cleaner, a video shop, a florist, and a walk-in beer cooler. And they have some groceries.

But as I walked through the miles of aisles, I realized what they didn't have, and what they need. A chaplain. I'm still working out the details, but it could really and truly make it a full-service experience. Because of the layout of the place, they will always be guaranteed many lost souls. There could be a confessional for those with compulsive shopping habits. Collection could be received thirty-four places by cash, check, or charge. Weddings would be a cinch with the bride coming down an aisle with flowers gathered up from the florist and the reception planned for the deli. Funerals I'm not so sure about, but it certainly would give a whole new meaning to "checking out."

I'm not ready to give up my day job, but when one hears the call, one must answer. Or was that just a price check?

Spirit of Life,

We sense your presence in our lives and in the connections we form with one another.

We seek not to ask for blessings withheld,

But rather for the insight to recognize blessings already bestowed, the humility of gratitude, and the wisdom to praise.

This food has already been blessed by nature's gift of sun and soil and rain.

We feel the blessings of those whose love embraces us always.

Our spirits are blessed by the tears and laughter that come to us from every opportunity to learn and love.

May these hidden blessings be felt among us now.

Amen. Shalom. May it be so.

No one lives in Syracuse, New York, for long without finding some way to make peace with winter. Snow is what we manufacture the most around here. It mixes with falling leaves early in November and dukes it out with the daffodils in April. I know what to expect, yet I am never ready.

When I woke to six inches the other day, I muttered about in search of gloves and a hat and scraper for the car before starting out to an early appointment. I was lost in thought about possible delays to a flight I was scheduled to take, the need for new tires, the urgency to get the storm windows in place, the leaves raked, and the garden mulched. All the standard winter worries. Then like a gong awakening me, a snow ball splashed against metal. I thought some kids had chosen my car as a handy target, but I soon saw that it was the stop sign that had been hit. I looked around to see the culprit. There he was, grinning broadly, rubbing his hands together in pride over his bulls-eye. A fellow about eighty years old. He waved. I waved. He smiled. I smiled.

I had a feeling he knew something about winter that I could stand to learn. By the time my appointment was over, most of the snow had melted. I had missed my chance to welcome winter. With a little practice, I'll have learned something by April.

There is a great deal of talk at Easter about the promise of eternal life, and the role that a proper faith can
play in overcoming death. We in the liberal church run
those words through our own translation devices to
grasp the promises of immortality given to all, not only
to those with a set of particular doctrinal beliefs. We
speak of the natural order of the seasons, of the contri-
butions we make that will outlive us, of the progres-
sion from one generation to the next. A lot of the time
this discussion satisfies me. Much of the time it seems
like enough.

A lot of what gets said in churches about Easter is
"Theo-Talk," which is very interesting if you are a theo-
logian, but somewhat remote if you are just a regular
trying-as-hard-as-you-can-to-hold-it-together-worrying-
about-the bills/kids/parents-watching-your-weight/cho-
lesterol/blood pressure-working-to-keep-love-alive kind
of person. The theologians usually speak of getting
more time (which I think, frankly, misses the point
about Easter entirely)—when you may be feeling like,
"Eternal life? You've *got* to be kidding!"

Still, there are moments when I couldn't agree more
with Woody Allen when he says, "Some people want
to achieve immortality through their work or their de-
scendants. I want to achieve immortality by not dying."
There are those times when meaning emerges from ev-
erydayness, when something miraculous occurs, when

our eyes are opened, and we are suddenly overcome with a feeling that draws us into a passionate embrace with this life. In my book, *that's* immortality.

We've all touched some immortal thing in the world that requires us to make it real. Love. Beauty. Justice. Kindness. Trust. Compassion. Acceptance. All of these ideals are immortal, but they are manifest only if we give them form and flesh and bones to walk the earth. We don't need immortality; immortality needs us.

So in the Easter season of reawakening and renewal, do your part for immortality! Leave the theologians to carry on about the "ologies": eschatology, christology, teleology, and ontology. Listen instead to the poet who said, "Teach us to number our days that we may get a heart of wisdom." (Psalm 90:12)

I've always thought that Jesus makes a better hero than he does a God. I'll take a hero with flaws any day over a perfect God. I'll take a hero that lives and dies in the world I know, over a God that's capable of transcending the limits of time and space that hold the rest of us earthbound. I'll take the mythology of the hero whose life allows him or her to transcend death, over the theology of the God that never could die, that would never share the passage we take.

At Easter, I find plenty of cause to celebrate. Not the heroic in God, though. After all, how hard can it be for God to be a hero? But I do celebrate the heroic possibilities that I have witnessed in human souls, when through resurrections of our own fashioning, we rise.
Rise to hope,
Rise to love,
Rise to heal,
Rise to forgive,
Rise to courage,
Rise to foolishness,
Rise to wisdom,
Rise, even to die.
But most essentially, to rise to life.
Not to die a hero, but to live as one.
May we rise to Life.

In the spirit of our living tradition we find ourselves together in a place made sacred by the presence of both the holy and the human, brought together in this space and in this time, through our meeting.

We are here to worship together . . .
To sing and to pray,
To be still and to be alert,
to encounter the exquisite treasures of being present in this moment where hope and vision speak most clearly.
We are here to celebrate together . . .
To see in others their best,
To dream together of a world of justice,
To hold hands and hug,
To acknowledge hurt and to seek to heal.

We are here, all of us, to grasp a glimmer of the calling that is ours alone in this world. To hear the whispered words that are spoken only for us, that give us all the clues we need to answer the call we were created for. The messengers of our common calls come always in disguise. Spoken to us by chance, by the soul, by the wind, by times of trouble, by our joy. They are rarely silent. We can't escape them. They wait, always patient, for us. Even now.

Let us begin our worship.
Let us begin our celebration.
Let us begin to listen for the calling that awaits us and invites us to live our truth.
Let us begin.

Last month there was an ecumenical celebration in which I chose not to participate. Normally, we religious liberals seem game to sample the smorgasbord of all sorts of spiritual traditions. A hint of Hinduism, a jot of Judaism, a bit of Buddhism, an iota of Islam, a pinch of paganism. But this particular event made my stomach a little queasy. It was billed as "The Week of Prayer for Christian Unity."

On the surface it sounds innocuous enough. The history of the institutional Christian church has been one of endless schisms and divisions, resulting in dozens of denominations that claim to be "the one true faith." That of course is how the original two denominations of our religious heritage either emerged or were evicted from the established churches of the early nineteenth century. Their heresies disturbed the unity of the religious monopoly helped by the state-supported Congregational Church, established by the Pilgrims seeking religious freedom. (For themselves alone, apparently.) Our own history makes a case against the shape of conformity that unity tends to take when it becomes an institutional objective.

A little unity might be a novel approach by religious people in general, but when Christians start talking about it, I get nervous. A letter came to me from a group of clergy in town asking for my help in promoting censorship of TV programming. It closed with the promise that "when Christians take a stand together, there's no stopping us." That's what I'm afraid of.

If a good dose of Christian disunity allows women to keep control of their reproductive rights, allows public education to be free of religious practice, allows art and literature to be free of censorship, keeps the definition of private and personal morality out of the hands of the church, and continues to promote the confusion and questioning that allows new visions of truth to emerge, then I'm all for it.

Perhaps you might keep their disharmony in your prayers, or I will keep it in mine.

The sign on the door said "Closed for Business," yet the images in my memory were very much open and alive.

The Westcott Variety Store had gone out of business. For decades it was an institution in that little business district just east of the university. Now it had gone the way of jacks, penny candy, and the hula hoop, although it's a safe bet that those items were still in stock on the day the store closed. The Westcott Variety store had everything you needed, and a good number of things you couldn't ever possibly imagine needing, jammed into narrow aisles.

Now it was empty, barren. I stood at the window, looking in. What I saw was more than my reflection; I saw a good deal of my past.

I would guess my memories of that place are "pre-conscious." During my first year of life we lived just a few blocks away, and my mother tells of dragging me and my brother on a sled to the store on errands. As I grew up, the Westcott Variety Store was the place we went each year to pick out characters and creatures to augment the featured players in our family creche. They are not very beautiful, at least to my adult aesthetic sense, but they were the greatest thing to a child.

The Westcott Variety Store was the kind of place a kid could go with a meager allowance and feel wealthy. It was a good place to buy a present for your grand-mother. The search for birthday party favors began and ended in the bins by the front counter, divided by glass, full of marvelous trinkets.

It was July when we moved back to Syracuse a few years ago. I wanted window boxes, but all the garden supply stores were out of stock. In a moment of inspiration, I knew who to call. Not only did the Westcott Variety Store have window boxes, they had a choice of sizes and colors as well. It has been said, and it may be true, that it was impossible *not* to find what you wanted there.

The Westcott Variety Store remained the antithesis of the modern store to its closing day. Perhaps that is why it couldn't last. One does not get rich selling corn-cob pipes, mouse traps, and wooden clothespins. So, like a lot of things we have come to let go of, we realize that we have been enriched for a time by people and places that must eventually live only in the realm of memory. It is a worthy reminder to take a close look at those things we treasure while we still have the chance. It won't make them last any longer. But it can give them the permanence that lets them be seen in the reflection of a plate glass window of an empty store by a busy street on a summer day.

"To be nobody-but-yourself—in a world which is doing its best, night and day, to make you everybody else— means to fight the hardest battle which any human being can fight; and never stop fighting."

—E. E. Cummings,
from "A Poet's Advice to Students"

I don't know where I read it—the headline, "Boy Raised By Wolves!" Maybe there was a picture of a hairy creature lurking in the woods. Maybe there was a dead rabbit at his feet. Maybe it was more fiction than fact. But the gist of it was that this child, raised by wolves, had become one.

I don't think so.

Yes, he may have learned how wolves act. Indeed, he may have lacked human language. No doubt he felt safer in the world he had been taught to survive in, even if it was not his own. But he wasn't a wolf, even if he had the wolves fooled.

I think of that story every time I hear people talking about everything from the need to make gay and lesbian people into something they are not, to urging us to just "be quiet" about it. These people are usually the ones who reject the idea of gay pride as somehow self-indulgent. The way I figure it, I had excellent training to be a heterosexual. Some outstanding heterosexuals have shaped and guided my life. My parents are straight. My relatives are straight. My neighbors were straight. My teachers were straight. My ministers were straight. My coaches were straight. But I am not. And believe me, I've tried. I'm one of the many "raised by heterosexuals."

Like the boy raised by wolves, I figured out how to survive against my nature. It's all I saw. It's all I knew. Like him, I didn't have access to the language of my being. No one around me was speaking it. And I too had the wolves fooled. In fact, I even fooled myself.

I thank the heterosexuals who raised me. They did the best they could with what they had to work with. But they can stop trying now. That's what gay pride is all about. It's a kind of crash course in survival techniques for those of us whose basic training in life no longer works. No one taught us what we would need to know when we were young. We must teach each other to trust the deep instincts and true impulses of our souls. When enough of us have done that, perhaps the world will be safer for the boys and the girls, like me, who must find their way home by another way.

There is a fellow who shares my surname, yet with whom I have no relation, who has made a fortune writing books that are pitched as guides to success in any number of fields. It all started with the volume entitled "The One-Minute Manager." It's been a bestseller and has spawned several sequels that have made the other Mr. Blanchard a millionaire. I've been contemplating a book called, "The One-Minute Marriage," not to describe failed relationships, but offering a nifty program to marital bliss through sixty-second solutions. I know there is a market, but I have only been able to think of one thing that could be confined to the current cultural attention span of a minute. Just one, and that's if I talk fast.

There are some weighty obstacles. For one, in a marriage, unlike the world of business and management, you cannot delegate the hard work. You have to do it yourselves. And second, the key elements to happiness in any relationship are always changing. Today we need a great sense of humor. Tomorrow what's required is forgiveness. The day after that, maybe a spirit of playfulness. And on and on. At weddings I often feel couples expect me to offer some sage advice that will enrich their marriage. The fact is, I haven't a clue what it is they'll need. Most of the time I'm not so sure what I need in my most intimate relationships.

I often leave my counsel to this: Do more than simply keep the promises made in your vows. Do something more: keep promising. As time passes, keep promising new things, deeper things, vaster things, yet-unimagined things. Promises that will be needed to fill the expanses of time and of love. To keep promising, you won't need a license, you won't need witnesses, you won't need a minister. You will only need what you already have: each other.

Keep promising . . .

Did you know that July is National Hot Dog Month? It
is. It is also National Eye Exam Month, Minority Tour-
ism Month, Hitchhiking Month, National Baked Bean
Month, National Ice Cream Month, National July Be-
longs to Blueberries Month, National Lamb and Wool
Month, National Peach Month, National Picnic Month,
National Purposeful Parenting Month, National Recreation and Parks Month, National Tennis Month, Sports
and Recreation Books Month, and it is also National
Anti-Boredom Month. There seems to be something for
everyone. I figure I'll do my part in celebrating about
half of these commemorations before the month is out.
A picnic with a well-stacked cooler would take care of
many, and if you hitchhiked to the park in a wool
sweater and brought a book about sports and an op-
tometrist along you'd be well on your way to a thor-
ough celebration of July. The only festival I plan to omit
from my July is the last one mentioned: National
Anti-Boredom Month. I think July is a wonderful time
to be bored.

In spite of what they hold as true at The Boring In-
stitute of Maplewood, New Jersey, summertime is the
ideal season for boredom. Some people call it vacation.
I think being bored is an undervalued state of mind.
Obviously, it's not a place one wants to stay all the time,
but only when you're bored do you let yourself fully
pay attention. When you're a kid that's when you lie

on the ground and watch the industry of ants, or look for shapes in the clouds, or find four leaf clovers, or make up a game with whoever's hanging around. Later on in life, it's when, well, it's when you do the same sort of stuff. But while you're watching the ants or scouring the skies, you're also imagining all kinds of other things, making connections, sorting out your life, sensing the patterns that give your life its shape. That doesn't happen when you're in a hurry. It doesn't happen when every day has a full agenda. Those things rarely happen when you want to make them happen.

Boredom is one of those gifts life gives us that we often think we'd just as soon do without, and it would surely be a curse if it was unrelieved. But for most of us, it's a temporary state of grace that we visit from time to time, temporarily without our bearings, when we discover all the ways we human creatures are made for wonder.

As summer arrives, I anticipate a good boring July. This is our opportunity for authentic boredom. After all, everyone knows August is National Canning Month, so you know we'll be busy then.

"I have spent my days stringing and unstringing my instrument while the song I came to sing remains unsung."

—Rabindranath Tagore

On sabbatical in East Africa, I heard a story of a people who believe that we are each created with our own song. Their tradition as a community is to honor that song by singing it as welcome when a child is born, as comfort when the child is ill, in celebration when the child marries, and in affirmation and love when death comes. Most of us were not welcomed into the world in that way. Few of us seem to know our song.

It takes a while for many of us to figure out which is our song, and which is the song that others would like us to sing. Some of us are slow learners. I heard my song not necessarily from doing extraordinary things in exotic places, but also from doing some pretty ordinary things in some routine places. For every phrase I heard climbing Kilimanjaro, I learned another in a chair in a therapist's office. For every measure I heard in the silence of a retreat, I heard another laughing with my girls. For every note I heard in the wind on the beach at Lamu, I gleaned more from spending time with a dying friend as her children sang her song back to her. What came to astound me was not that the song appeared, but that it was always there.

I figure that the only way I could have known it for my own was if I had heard it before, before memory went to work making sense and order of the mystery of our beginning. Our songs sing back to us something of our essence, something of our truth, something of our uniqueness. When our songs are sung back to us, it is not about approval, but about recognizing our being and our belonging in the human family.

It is good to know our songs by heart for those lonely times when the world is not singing them back to us. That's usually a good time to start humming to yourself, that song that is most your own.

They can be heard as songs of love or of longing, songs of encouragement or of comfort, songs of struggle or of security. But most of all, they are the songs of life, giving testimony to what has been, giving praise for all we're given, giving hope for all we strive for, giving voice to the great mystery that carries each of us in and out of this world.

Dear Julia and Emily,

I'm Life. You don't know me, but I know you. I was here before you were born, and I will be here after you have died, but without you I wouldn't exist. We need each other. You count in the greater scheme of things, but even I don't know what it is you will give to the world you've been born into. That's something you'll need to figure out. You'll get some clues from me, and your parents, and those who love you, but you are the ones who will decide to what dark corners of the world you'll bring light and love. You don't have to be Jesus, or Buddha, or Mother Theresa. You just have to be you.

At times, just being you will create problems. It's a trial and error process. There will be people who would prefer that you were "them" instead of "you," and that gets confusing. You will do some things that will make your parents unhappy, but you can assume they did the same to their own parents, so don't let that take you off the path that is yours. Parents are not generally programmed to understand their children, but rather to keep them safe, and warm and dry, and mostly loved, and eventually to let them grow and go. If you are parents someday, this will be clearer. Until such time, trust me on this one.

You will lose things this year. A toy, a ring, a kite. It's going to keep happening, and to things more important to you than toys and rings and kites. There will be people, and dreams, and jobs, and homes, and traditions that will mean the world to you that will pass out of your grasp. Sometimes there are ways to hold on, but not usually. They can't be kept. You get to keep memories and all the hard-earned lessons that come from caring and loving and letting go. The ages have determined that it's better to feel very passionate about the most important parts of life, and come to reckon with the pain of loss, than to sacrifice the deepest feelings you can know. You don't get to have one without the other.

In the year to come you will discover things you never dreamed of before. My specialty is variety and innovation. I make sure you never have to worry about finding something new and even amazing to discover. Some call them miracles, but they're really rather ordinary. The miracle is the process—not the object—of discovery.

It's all quite astounding when you get right down to it. Even when you grow old the snow will chill your skin, and the green of spring will be there to dazzle you, and with any luck there will be someone whose embrace will give you comfort and love. They will be no less wonderful over time. In fact, some of them get even better.

Have a good year. I'll write again next year. I promise.
Love,
    Life